Surrey at Work

IN OLD PHOTOGRAPHS

The start of working life. This indenture was issued to Alfred Adley of Thames Ditton High Street in 1899 when he started his apprenticeship at the Thames Ditton statue foundry. The owners of the foundry at this time, Arthur Hollinshead and Artur Burton, have both signed the document which stated that the apprenticeship would last for seven years. Wages during this period are specified, rising from five shillings per week during the first two years to the princely sum of fifteen shillings a week in the seventh. The foundry went on to achieve greatness, producing many statues of the famous for cities around the world. The busiest period of the foundry's life, however, was tinged with sadness. Following the First World War, the order book was filled with requests for war memorials for towns and villages throughout the country.

Surrey at Work

IN OLD PHOTOGRAPHS

Compiled by
CHRIS SHEPHEARD

ALAN SUTTON

SIHG
Surrey Industrial History Group

Alan Sutton Publishing Limited
Phoenix Mill · Far Thrupp
Stroud · Gloucestershire

First published 1992

Copyright © 1992 Chris Shepheard
and Glenys Crocker

Published in collaboration with the
Surrey Industrial History Group.

DEDICATION: To the many unknown
photographers of yesteryear, who have
left us all such a wealth of fine images of
our county.

**British Library Cataloguing
in Publication Data**

Shepheard, Chris
Surrey at Work in old photographs
I. Title
942.21

ISBN 0-7509-0127-6

Typeset in 9/10 Sabon.
Typesetting and origination by
Alan Sutton Publishing Limited.
Printed in Great Britain by
The Bath Press, Avon.

Ready for the day's work are these three steam rollers and their crews of the Epsom Rural District Council. The machines were built by Aveling and Porter of Rochester, Kent. All three carry the company's horse and 'Invicta' logo, and the leading roller appears to have a scarifier attached to the rear for tearing up the old road surface. The gas lamp has an unusual twist in its column in order to get some light around the corner of the brick wall on the right.

Contents

Introduction

In the middle of the nineteenth century, when the photographic record was just beginning, the historian of Surrey, E.W. Brayley, described the county of his day. He compared its inhabitants with those of England as a whole and with the people of Middlesex, which then included London north of the Thames. Surrey at that time occupied the south bank, from Egham in the west through Kingston, Wandsworth and Southwark to Rotherhithe in the east. The county was judged to be considerably below the average in agriculture and not much above it in manufacturing, handicrafts and trades. However, on the basis of the number of 'educated men, independent persons and number of domestic servants', it was considerably higher in 'wealth, intelligence and comfort' – though inferior to its sophisticated northern neighbour.

Brayley published his *Topographical History of Surrey* in 1850 and his appendix on the population of the county and its occupations was based upon the census returns of 1841. He gave an account of the manufacturing industries of the time – brewing, distilling, hat making, leather, paper, cotton printing and bleaching, chemicals, glass and pottery, machinery, and printing. It is significant that all his examples were close to London, since most of the economic development and population growth of Surrey in the nineteenth century was in the northern, metropolitan part of the county, in those districts which have since been absorbed by the capital.

Through successive changes in local government, Surrey has lost about a fifth of its original area since 1889, when the former London County Council was formed, though it gained part of Middlesex, the future borough of Spelthorne, in 1965. The first task therefore in compiling a historical book about the county is to decide which boundary to use. In this collection of old photographs, the principle which has been followed is that the scene should have been in Surrey when the picture was taken. The tremendous influence of London is thereby duly recognized and represented, as well as the varied aspects of life beyond the metropolitan part of the county.

London's influence has been felt most strongly in the physical spread of the built-up area and the growth of commuter suburbs farther out, with the network of roads and railways which serve them. But long before the explosion of urban development towards the end of the nineteenth century, many of the well-to-do of London looked to Surrey as a desirable place of residence, combining a convenient proximity to the capital with a landscape of tranquillity and charm. Apart from the royal palaces of Tudor times – Nonsuch and Oatlands, both now disappeared – Surrey has never had the very largest and grandest residences in the country, but many fine houses nevertheless. They include the important renaissance mansion of Sutton Place, and later houses such as Clandon, Claremont and Pains Hill. More significant though for the county's working population has been the spread of numerous more modest country houses and gardens which needed large numbers of domestic servants and tradesmen for their running and upkeep.

The capital has also looked to surrounding areas for provisions and services of many kinds. Surrey has provided sites for reservoirs, hospitals for the mentally ill and handicapped, and a vast Victorian cemetery at Woking, while Surrey farmers and market gardeners have long supplied food for the London markets.

Something of the variety and richness of life in London can also be seen in Surrey, in many interesting and unusual industries which have been established. Some of these are represented in this book, such as the Liberty textile printing works at Merton, peppermint distilleries at Banstead, a wax refinery and the Monotype works at Redhill, a statue foundry at Thames Ditton, whose products went all over Britain and the Empire, and a factory making poppies for Remembrance.

Away from metropolitan Surrey life was very different. Much of the county is farmland but heavy clay lands in the south have been covered by woodland and poor sandy soils in the west have supported only heaths. These areas, around Bagshot and Hindhead, were crossed by main roads from London to the south and west of England notorious for highwaymen. It was found, however, that the light sandy soils were easy to work and when manured were ideal for raising plants, and from the late eighteenth century many nursery gardens were established around Woking and Bagshot. The heaths also provided ideal sites for army camps and training grounds. The town of Camberley developed around military establishments, the Sandhurst Royal Military College of 1812 at York Town and the Staff College of 1862 at Cambridge Town.

The wooded south of the county, with its coppices and charcoal burners, was part of an important industrial region until the eighteenth century when heavy industry moved to the coalfields of the North and Midlands. The Wealden iron industry died out, as did the glass industry which in the Middle Ages and in Tudor times flourished around Chiddingfold. Surrey also had a woollen industry which was well-known for its 'Guildford blue' cloth, dyed with woad, but this too died out, largely in the seventeenth century.

Other early industries have survived until more recent times and are featured in the photographs. Gunpowder was made in Surrey from the sixteenth century onwards, and its manufacture was continued at Chilworth near Guildford until 1920. Paper mills appeared in the county in the seventeenth century and the last one closed at Godalming in the 1920s. Another old Surrey industry, leather manufacture, continued at Gomshall until the 1980s while the knitwear industry, which came to Surrey in the seventeenth century, has survived in the county up to the present day.

Chalk pits and limeworks are a striking feature of the Surrey landscape and have provided employment in towns and villages along the North Downs. Stone quarries around Merstham and Reigate produced building stone in the Middle Ages and hearthstone for cleaning floors in more recent times. Sand extraction has been an important industry throughout the long outcrop of sandstone which runs eastwards across the width of the county from Farnham. Clay has been used for pottery making near Farnham, and has been dug for brick making in many localities, often to serve immediate local needs. Large modern brickworks are still active on the Wealden clays in the south of the county.

From the late nineteenth century onwards many new industries developed based on new technology, particularly in the field of engineering. Important developments occurred in Surrey, especially in early motoring and aviation, for which the motor circuit and airfield at Brooklands became world famous.

The Surrey Industrial History Group, whose members have compiled this book, is expressly concerned with researching the history of industry in the county and with recording, and when appropriate preserving, its physical remains. One aspect of the Group's work is the locating and collecting of old pictorial records. This book aims to make these more widely available and to encourage others to save and care for any old photographs in their possession. The scope has been widened from pictures of industry to the whole field of work, so it includes not only manufacturing, farming, quarrying, and all the aspects of transport, but public and social services, domestic work, retail trades and entertainment.

The pictures are arranged according to themes, partly determined by the kind of material which happens to survive. The first set, entitled 'The Job in Hand', shows people at work on a variety of tasks, while the section 'Everything Stopped for the Camera' is a reflection of the fact that people did, more often than not, cease whatever interesting business they were engaged in and pose to have their picture taken. 'The Workplace' has been compiled from the many pictures which survive of the premises where people worked. 'The Working Man and Woman' is a collection of pictures primarily of people, and 'Women at Work' highlights the jobs which women undertook in wartime. 'Keeping the Wheels Turning' deals with the large subject of transport. 'Accidents will Happen' reflects the newsworthiness of its subject matter, with fire-fighting and traffic accidents having a particular appeal. 'It Pays to Advertise' illustrates the value of old advertisements as a record of former times, and finally 'Technology's Edge' shows some of the new and progressive endeavours which have taken place in Surrey.

The oldest images in the book are from well before the age of photography, and show a carrier and candlemaker depicted on trade tokens from around 1640. The oldest photograph dates from around 1865 and shows St Catherine's ferry across the River Wey at Guildford. In general the book covers the period up to about the 1960s, when industries left their old locations, town centres began to be redeveloped and another generation of industries grew up in modern trading estates. Some traditional industries, however, are still alive and the latest photograph shows a miller dressing his millstones at Coltsford Mill near Oxted, the last working watermill in the county, in 1978.

Many people have helped in the production of this book. The SIHG's Patron, the artist David Shepherd, has contributed a painting of the engine sheds at Guildford Station. Other members of the Group have played their part, and many members of local history societies, and indeed of the general public, have responded to appeals for old photographs. It is hoped that the publication of this collection will encourage many more to come forward so that a second volume can be compiled.

Glenys Crocker, Castle Arch, Guildford

8

SECTION ONE
The Job in Hand

For centuries the economy of Surrey was largely agricultural. Large parts of the county were used for sheep rearing and were famous for wool-based industries. Hurdles were a vital requirement for the shepherd and, when this photograph was taken around the turn of the century, were made throughout the county in specially coppiced woodland. The hurdle maker is believed to be working in Rowledge near Farnham.

Two scenes depicting life in the early 1900s at Milton Farm, Westcott. That above shows haymaking in progress using large rakes and pitchforks under the watchful eye of the farmer. Below, a waggon and team pause for the photographer in Milton Street. All the waggons bear the names of the farmers Kent and Chalke as well as the name of the farm itself.

Agriculture has always played a major part in the economy of rural Surrey. In the shadow of Reigate Hill around 1906 a ploughman turns his team at the end of the furrow on what was probably part of Colley Farm. Notice the harrow lying on the ground beyond the plough.

The chicken grubbing for worms at Nutley Dene Farm, Charlwood, seems undisturbed by the rick thatcher working above. Note the staddle stones on which the rick is built, designed to keep rats and other rodents from the grain stored above. They also seem to be providing a home for a family of ducks.

Lavender production at Mitcham spanned agricultural and industrial processes. The crop being harvested above in one of Miller's fields, was grown throughout the district and transported to the banks of the River Wandle for distillation of the essential oils, seen below in a drawing dating from around 1840.

Over the years peppermint has been grown over a large area of north Surrey. This crop could only be grown in a field for five years before new land was needed. One of the firms involved was W.J. Machell's of Banstead. Left, the still is being loaded in the 1950s and, below, Mr Machell, on the left, examines the resulting peppermint oil. The company also grew and distilled lavender.

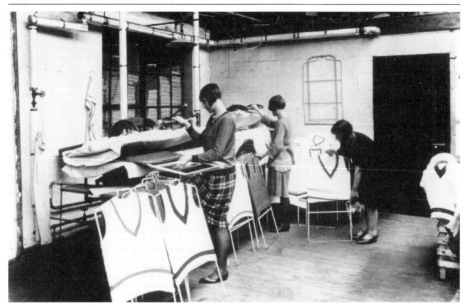

Knitwear was a major industry in Godalming for many years, the firm of Pitchers being one of the best known. William Pitchers was outfitter to Charterhouse School and his wife Lucy ran a drapery and millinery shop. She was also responsible for starting the knitting business and introduced new methods of making patterned sweaters by machine. Here, sweaters are being put on wire frames ready for the steam presses in 1930. At this time the company produced their own gas for heating and lighting on the premises.

Another firm which had its own gas retort was Swabey and Saunders of Ashtead. Two of the firm's employees are seen charging the plant in about 1910.

Archaeologists at work on the Roman villa discovered in Ashtead Woods during August 1925 by Anthony Lowther. Material from the villa is believed to have been incorporated in the nearby Saxon church of St Giles which is set in its own triangular earthwork.

There certainly was a job in hand for this group of navvies at the turn of the century, somewhere in the Redhill area. It is obvious that they are shoring up and clearing an earth bank, but the purpose is unknown. The shoring appears to be made of old railway sleepers so perhaps it was to protect the sides of a new railway cutting.

One of the more unusual crops of Surrey is watercress, its centre of production being the village of Abinger Hammer. A group of the local workers pose with some of the freshly picked cress sometime around 1880.

The industry is still very much a going concern, with restaurants in the picturesque village offering watercress teas and the very refreshing watercress soup. Those employed in raising the crop must have been very hardy individuals for much of their working life was spent standing ankle deep in running water. These two photographs taken around 1949 show cutting the cress, left, and cleaning the beds after the harvest, above. The latter is very important and the growing of cress is governed by strict rules which ensure that water-borne diseases are not transmitted.

At ten minutes to nine on a wet morning in 1938 the mail is loaded aboard a British Airways Lockheed Electra at Croydon Airport. The American Electra had a special mail compartment in the nose, and this aircraft was bound for Scandinavia. British Airways should not be confused with the current airline of that name; it was one of the fore-runners, along with Imperial Airways, of the British Overseas Airways Corporation which later merged with British European Airways to form the current British Airways in 1974.

This idyllic scene belies an irksome task on the Wey Navigation, for these men are hand dredging the cut. They are using very long handled scoops to raise the sediment into the narrow boat for transport to the dumping ground. It would take several days to clear even a small section of the channel and the men obviously travelled to the site each day by bicycle, one of which can be seen propped against the nearby telegraph pole.

Many Surrey mills have produced paper at some time during their history, but few on the scale of Woking Mill when this photograph was taken in the early 1890s. Paper pulp was fed to the left-hand end of the machine and emerged on the large heated drum, while the device tended by apprentices to the right slit the rolled paper into sheets.

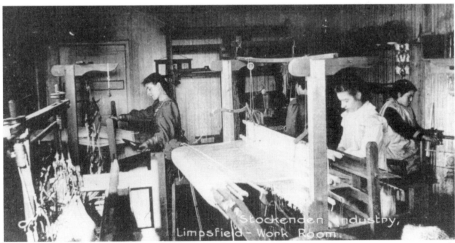

These young ladies from Limpsfield appear to be working in a domestic living-room with little room for manoeuvre around the four looms at which they work. Stockenden is believed to be the name of the house in which they are working, for a fifteenth-century house of that name exists today just south of the village. This photograph, taken around 1908, gives a very good idea of the crowded workroom conditions of the day.

Gunsmiths at work, probably during the 1920s, in Jeffery's workshops in Guildford. The company, who made as well as serviced guns, are still in business today from their shop in the High Street, although their trade now encompasses a much wider range of sports.

A machine-gun detachment of the 1st Battalion of the Queen's Regiment 'on manoeuvres' at Lingfield around 1913, keenly watched by members of the local populace.

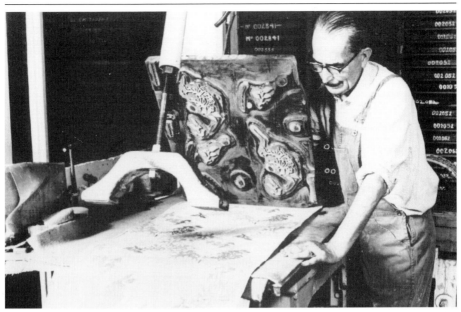

William Morris founded his model factory at Merton in 1881. His idea was to revive the hand crafts which were rapidly disappearing in the age of the machine. In an old Huguenot silk-weaving factory he set up facilities for the design and production of carpets, tapestries, wallpaper and stained glass. In the top photograph a craftsmen is applying the fourth of eight colours to a Sanderson wallpaper in Morris's 'Seaweed' design, while below D.W. Griffiths works on the tapestry 'La Pomana' in 1936.

Many places in the county have clay suitable for the production of bricks and, starting in the late fifteenth century, hundreds of small brickworks have appeared and disappeared over the years. Here are two brickfields at the foot of the North Downs between Guildford and Dorking, *c.* 1900. The large group above are standing around the horse gin used to mix the clay at Whitedown brickworks, Abinger, while the brickmaker and apprentice (bottom opposite) are at the appropriately named Kiln Meadow, Westcott.

Swallow Tiles at Cranleigh still produce tiles in the way they have since the works were established in 1894. The sand-faced tiles have a rough, weathered appearance with variations in colour and are used largely in the repair and restoration of old buildings.

In East Surrey the Upper Greensand beds have been worked for centuries to produce firestone and hearthstone. These two sandstones obviously had connections with fireplaces. Firestone was originally used in the building of chimneys and hearths, but later became widely used in the glass-making industry. Its precise use is unknown but was believed to be for holding plate glass flat while it was ground and polished. Hearthstone, however, has no such enigmas about its use: it was used as raw lumps, or ground and compressed into small blocks, for application to domestic stone steps, window sills and hearths as a whitening agent. Here are two photographs of the hearthstone works of Reigate Mines Ltd in the 1930s. The lower photograph shows the material being made into blocks ready for sale to shops while, above, one of the horses and its handler pose by a block of hearthstone fresh from the mine.

Mechanization eventually reached farms everywhere, and here we see what probably represented the changeover in 1905 at Clifton's Field, Reigate. Harvesting by hand using a scythe or sickle and hook must have been a laborious and tiring process, but it was probably with mixed feelings that the labourers welcomed the horse-drawn reaper and binder, as it undoubtedly meant that the work-force would be reduced.

In the 1900s this barn in Bookham was moved on rollers, mainly by muscle power, and turned through ninety degrees. The purpose of all this effort is seen below, for it was jacked up to form the top storey of the house then named Pitscottie. It survives today but has been renamed The Moorings. This was not the only re-use of a barn in Bookham at this time, for the Bird family of the Grange presented one to the village in 1906. Located in Church Road, it forms the centre of village activities as the Barn Hall.

The restoration of old buildings is not just a modern art: over the centuries, thankfully, people have always wanted to preserve reminders of the past. This is the Guest House at Lingfield which originally formed part of a college founded by the third Lord Cobham in 1432. Restoration took place in the late 1890s under the direction of C. Forster Hayward, whose son bequeathed the building to Surrey County Council in 1954. It stands next to the church, forming part of an attractive group of half-timbered houses, and is used today as a library.

The development of St George's Hill, Weybridge, as a residential area was started in 1912 by W.G. Tarrant. Included in the scheme was an eighteen-hole golf course on what was dense woodland; this necessitated the felling of some 7,000 trees using traction engines. The stumps and roots were then removed using dynamite, as shown in the photograph.

Amid a carpenter's nightmare stands the gang of navvies engaged in the rebuilding of Papercourt Lock on the Wey Navigation downstream from Send. The work-force is large by today's standards for a job of this size, but at the turn of the century these men did not have the benefit of power tools.

During the 1950s many outlying communities had the benefit of mobile grocery shops. Tongham was no exception, being regularly visited by the Commer-powered Runfold Roadshop. It was obviously as popular with the children as with their mothers as it carried confectionery among the more mundane items.

The Monotype Company of Salfords near Redhill built composing machines for the printing industry. Their products were exported widely and therefore a large variety of different keyboards were needed. Here we see ladies at work in the 'keybank button store' in 1953. They are selecting the lettered plastic key tops from the drawers around them and positioning them in the trays for eventual fixing to the machine keyboards.

Demolition and preservation of historic buildings. The beautiful half-timbered house, below, in Oxted was demolished in 1908. Today it would probably have become a listed building, but the best that could have been hoped for this example was that parts were later re-used elsewhere. However, when the Cornmarket was closed in Guildford High Street the entrance was retained to form an impressive arched approach to the Tunsgate beyond. During 1936–7 (left) the columns of the portico were moved further apart in order to allow vehicles to pass through.

Everything Stopped for the Camera

The staff of Tongham sawmill gather for the camera with the tools of their trade at the end of the last century. Some of the yard's produce is stacked to the left on a waggon, and much of this was probably used in the building of nearby Aldershot Camp. A variety of cutting instruments is also to be seen, including hand and felling axes and single- and two-handed cross-cut saws, as well as the circular variety. The man fourth from the right in the front row appears to be holding an early adjustable spanner.

Surrey probably had more than its fair share of large country houses, each of which required a large staff to run. Bury Hill House at Dorking was in the ownership of the Quaker brewing family of Barclay from 1803 until 1952. These two photographs, taken around the turn of the century, show the gardeners (above) and the maintenance staff complete with dog (below).

More gardeners, this time at Moor Park House in Farnham, one-time home to Jonathan Swift. The date is probably during the 1880s, and the building still exists today albeit as a finishing school with a much reduced gardening staff.

A rather formal group of Dorking laundry staff at Cotmandene at the turn of the century.

Hammond's builders pause for the photographer in 1920 while building a wall in Tangier Road, Guildford, around the property of Fogwill's seed merchants.

Extractive industries always cause much controversy wherever they are located. At one time virtually the whole of Farnham south of the railway line was dug over for gravel from the river terraces. These workers are pausing from their labours at Wakeford's pit in Snailslynch in the 1920s, and include, from the left, 'Aurie' Parratt, Stamp, -?-, David Parratt, Gatterell and Stockham.

Nurses and patients of Caterham Cottage Hospital pose for the photographer in the well-kept gardens on 12 June 1903.

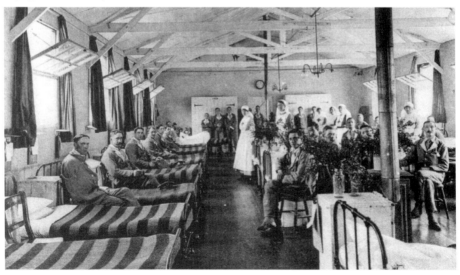

The Anderson family of Waverley Abbey House near Farnham turned the entire property into a military hospital for returning wounded during the First World War. Rob Roy Ward is seen here in 1914 with the inmates and staff positioned with military precision in one of several wooden buildings erected in the grounds. After the war the entire contents of the hospital were auctioned locally.

The interior of the bus garage in Onslow Street, Guildford, with mechanics posing with their charges. The double-decker is a 'B' Type which probably dates the photograph to just after the First World War. This building later became Jackson's Garage before demolition to make way for yet another multi-storey car park.

East Surrey Traction Company staff outside their Reigate garage in Bell Street around 1913. The bus was probably a newly delivered example as it bears no advertising boards as yet, unlike bus No. 5, below, with its crew in Victoria Road, Horley, at about the same time.

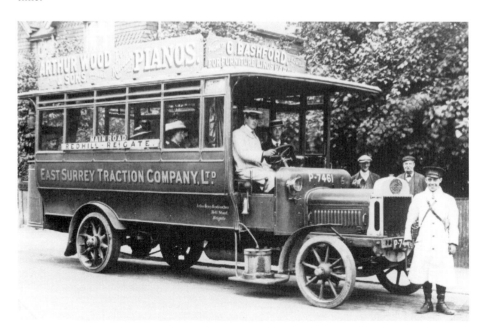

The firm of A. Harris and Sons at Wrecclesham Pottery near Farnham can trace the origins of its craft back to the Roman potteries established just over the Hampshire border in nearby Alice Holt forest, so the potters have every justification in feeling proud as they pose for the camera with some of their handiwork in the early 1900s.

Farnham was home to the famous chronicler of rural life George Sturt, whose family ran a wheelwright's shop in East Street. The staff pose outside the premises at the end of the nineteenth century. The workshop still exists but is now a showroom for luxury cars.

Blacksmiths pose outside their forges, above in Haslemere and below at Holden's forge in Cobham High Street. Among the services offered at the latter were horseshoeing, plumbing, fencing, gasfitting, wheelwrighting, implement repairs, and bell hanging.

At the vitreous enamel plant at Elm Works, Summerstown near Wimbledon in 1933 the staff pause from their task of enamelling light fittings. Piles of shades can be seen around the room in various stages of production, and the stove doors are visible on the left wall, one showing severe smoke staining on the wall above.

Fuller's Earth, a mineral with a myriad of uses, has been dug to the east of Redhill from at least the seventeenth century, and the Romans are reputed to have made use of it long before this. One of the first uses, which utilized its ability to remove grease and dust, was in the cleaning (fulling) of wool. More modern applications include the refining of North Sea crude oil, producing granules for carrying agricultural chemicals, foundry clays, cement for special applications, cosmetics, and the making of cat litter. The upper photograph shows some young visitors to a Nutfield pit standing by a boiler used in the drying process; workers are pausing at their workplace for the camera at the same location, below.

A contrast in transport in these two watermill photographs. The horse-drawn waggon is being loaded outside Wonham Mill on the Shag Brook between Reigate Heath and Betchwood in 1895. James Bailey, below, poses with his staff and transport fleet at Heath Mill on the Hedge Brook at Worplesdon near Guildford. Mr Bailey was the miller here until 1922, having rebuilt the mill in 1902 following a disastrous fire.

In the days when labour was relatively cheap, the work-force of Pimm's Upper Corn Mill on the River Wandle gather in the courtyard, *c.* 1885. There are at least thirty people in the photograph, and five fully laden waggons and teams. A sack is suspended from the lucam to the right-hand side of the main building, and the man to the right of centre is holding an oil can.

Coulsdon and Purley air-raid rescue team line up beside their transport during the Second World War. All carry service respirators and the lorry is loaded with stirrup pumps, ladders, wheelbarrows and various timber baulks for shoring up damaged buildings.

The work-force of two Farnham shops pose for the photographer outside their respective premises in the 1950s. Shepheard's was a general store and sub-post office on Station Hill which closed for business during the 1970s having originally been converted from a commercial hotel. Included in the group are three generations of the Shepheard family, with young Christopher in the centre and his grandfather, Thomas, immediately behind; mother and father, Alec and Muriel, are to the left. Standing in the left of the doorway is Miss Nellie Chandler who was responsible for the stationery counter. Rose's were, and still are, seedsmen, corn merchants and livestock feed specialists in East Street, albeit now in different premises. Gert Brooks is third from the left and manager Phil Lucas is eighth left; his responsibilities included visiting local farms to collect their orders.

Firemen and their appliances have always been much photographed. Those above are proudly sitting on their first 'engine' at Cobham in 1899. However, at Redhill, by the time their manual appliance was photographed on 25 May 1907, it was already well used, having been built in 1865. The horse-drawn machine remained in use here until 1914, by which time it was reported as 'showing the effect of wear and hard work'.

Building workers show off their handiwork. Above, houses in Freelands Road, Cobham, and, below, a warehouse in the Hart, Farnham. Note the wooden scaffolding secured with rope at Cobham, a far cry from the steel-framed building, shown during the foundation stone laying ceremony in September 1953, of the wholesale grocers William Kingham and Son.

SECTION THREE
The Workplace

A small Surrey car producer, one of whose products can be seen at the rear of this work-shop scene, was the Pilgrim Motor Company of Weydon Lane, Farnham. The photograph was taken in 1918 when car production had already ceased; the firm eventually turned over entirely to producing oil pumps, particularly for use in motor cycles.

DENNIS BROTHERS, Limited.

A new additional Factory now being erected which, when completed, will be employing upwards of four hundred workpeople.

To enable us to cope with the increasing demand for DENNIS MOTORS.

The building shown above is still in existence on the corner of Onslow Street and Bridge Street, Guildford, and is thought to be the oldest surviving multi-storey car factory in Europe and possibly the world. It was built for Dennis Brothers in 1901, less than a year after commencing business from the old barracks in Friary Street. However, by 1905 even this had proved inadequate and work had started on a new site on Woodbridge Hill. By the 1950s, when the lower photograph was taken, this had grown to cover some thirty-one acres. The firm is probably most famous for its fire engines, but also produced many other sorts of commercial vehicles, motor cars, cycles and lawnmowers.

Similar views of two very different industries at opposite ends of the county but with similar requirements of the natural elements. The view above, taken in the 1920s, shows Hale Laundry near Farnham. In the drying grounds can be seen the company's output drying and bleaching in the sun. At Redhill, below, are the premises of the British Wax Refining Company. Beeswax from all over the world is turned into a variety of wax and polish products here using locally produced Fuller's Earth for filtration. The wax is then bleached, now by chemical means, but in the 1930s when the photograph was taken, by exposure to the sun in open trays.

Two shops in North Street, Guildford, around 1925. The large drapery store of Gammons was built in 1895 while the ironmongery firm of Carling, Gill and Carling was established over two hundred years earlier. Neither firm is still in business.

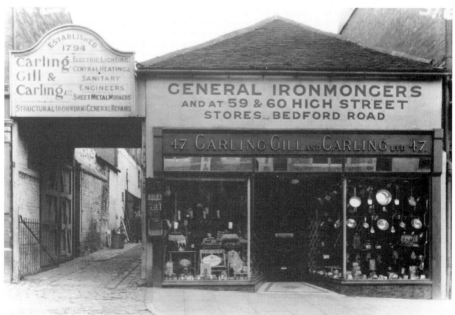

Two views of the Reigate Industrial and Provident Society's shop in Butter Hill off South Street, Dorking, taken in 1905. This was the first Co-operative store to come to the town, arriving in the previous year, 1904.

Haberdashery counters in two Surrey department stores, unstaffed, above, at White's store in Guildford High Street, where Marks and Spencer now stands, and, below, in Elphick's of Farnham which seems almost overstaffed. Notice the chairs provided for customers' use, now definitely a thing of the past.

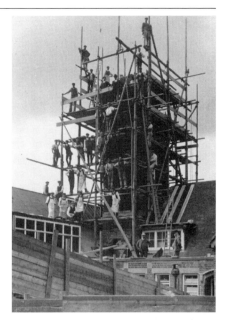

Crosby and Company, builders from Farnham, at work on a new clock tower for St John's Council School at Redhill in 1910.

These buildings in Haslemere High Street were demolished shortly after this photograph was taken on 6 March 1912, and the London County & Westminster Bank built on the site. The shops belonged to a hairdresser (behind the lamp-post), a boot and shoe store, Appleby's, and on the right Sydney Rogers' forage and corn merchants business with his transport fleet standing in the road outside.

Postmen hard at work sorting the morning's mail at Haslemere before setting off on their rounds.

An artist's view of the interior of Purnell's mineral water bottling plant in Onslow Street, Guildford. Clearly shown is the line-shafting which would have driven all the machinery in the factory from a central powerplant.

The Market Place, Kingston-on-Thames.

A contrast in markets between two of the major towns in the county reflecting their different locations. Kingston market, above, around the time of the First World War reflects its suburban surroundings, with stalls catering mainly for domestic requirements. Guildford, on the other hand, is very much a rural affair with the upper half of North Street taken over every week with livestock pens. The date is probably around 1880 and sheep predominate in this view. Stalls selling a variety of goods occupy the lower part of the street, a position they still retain today. The cattle market, however, moved many years ago, first to a site alongside Woodbridge Road and later to Slyfield Green.

The Sopwith company's aircraft production line at Ham near Richmond in 1918, with large numbers of fighters in manufacture for the Western Front. In 1920 Hawker Engineering took over the site and it is still in use by British Aerospace in 1992.

Hawker's used the airfield at Brooklands for erecting aeroplanes in the 1930s, and this view shows aircraft of the Hart/Hind/Audax series in production.

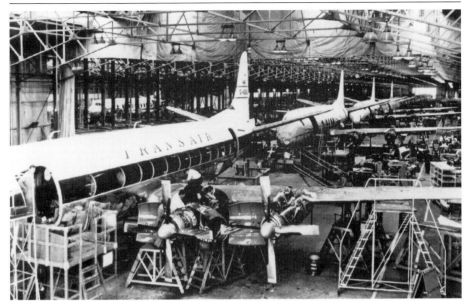

Brooklands airfield at Weybridge was the home of Vickers-Armstrong, who later became the British Aircraft Corporation. Probably their most famous product was the Wellington bomber, but after the Second World War production switched almost entirely to civilian aircraft. Above, Vickers Viscount 800s near completion and, below, VC10s for BOAC and British United Airways are being assembled in April 1964.

Before the advent of the jet engine every aeroplane needed at least one propeller. In the early days these were made of wood, in everything from back-street workshops to large factories. These two photographs epitomize the two extremes, that above believed to be near Farnham and the other a view of Lang's factory on Weybridge Trading Estate at Addlestone during the First World War.

In 1918 the royal family visited the works of Gordon Watney and Company at Addlestone who were engaged in the manufacture of aero engines. The royal party are seen inspecting the stores which held spares for Clerget engines.

A view of the finishing room at Alan Paine's Riverside Factory in Godalming. The company, which specializes in high quality, natural fibre sweaters mainly for the export market, established their works here in 1965. In 1991 production was moved elsewhere and the factory demolished to make way for a supermarket.

A massive army camp on Coulsdon Common during the First World War, *c.* 1915. The troops were probably on their way to the trenches of the Western Front, and one wonders how many ever saw these shores again.

One of innumerable gravel pits which have been worked at various times throughout the county. This one is at Farnham and shows an interesting variety of transport types, with Super Sentinel steam tipper lorry, narrow-guage railway hauled by a former War Department Light Railway 20 hp Motor Rail locomotive, and standard-gauge trucks at the Patterson pit's loading stage off Weydon Lane, and a freight train passing on the main line. Mr Thomas Patterson is believed to be the man wearing the trilby hat on the left of the photograph.

Thomas Penfold, Steam Masonry Works. Reigate.

Penfold's monumental masonry works were situated in Blackborough Road, Reigate, when this photograph was taken around 1909. The yard is well equipped to deal with quite large pieces of stone with its hoist, but quite what was steam-powered is not known, although it was probably the saw.

Dairy prams, and a bicycle for more express deliveries, are visible in this photograph of W.G. Davey's Horley Dairy, c. 1910, in the days before milk bottles. At this time the business was located in Station Road but moved later to the High Street. Notice the man using the cream separator in the centre and the apprentice scrubbing out a churn in the background.

A general view of the machine shop showing milling machines and miles of line-shafting and belting at the Monotype works at Salfords near Redhill in 1924. The company was established here in 1899 and the factory was built from bricks made of clay dug on site, the pit now forming an ornamental pond. During both World Wars the company produced large quantities of machine guns. Any health and safety inspector encountering the scene above today would promptly have a fit on sight of all the unguarded machinery.

Binscombe smithy near Godalming, probably around the turn of the century, with the blacksmith leaning on the stable door.

The coachbuilders in Ash were obviously kept very busy, and Hawkes & Horne, the bakers, were good customers. The site's connection with transport continued long after the coachbuilders' demise as Always Welding was established here, specializing in the conversion of commercial vehicles. Now the area has been redeveloped for housing.

Surrey watermills have had mixed fortunes. Cobham Mill, above, has been largely demolished for road widening, while Coxes Lock Mill on the Wey Navigation at Addlestone is now converted to luxury flats. The photograph shows grain barges awaiting unloading in the 1960s, but in previous centuries this had been an iron and silk mill. The present buildings date from 1901–06, and milling finally ceased here in 1983.

Right on the Surrey-Sussex border, at Shottermill near Haslemere was Pitford Mill. It served many purposes during its active life, including paper making and leather dressing, and after milling had ceased the buildings were used for the manufacture of fencing by the Stanley Underwood Company, as seen in this photograph taken in October 1911. The building has now been demolished and the site redeveloped for housing

Another Surrey watermill, this time at Chertsey and altogether more active, with the miller sitting at the upstairs doorway. This beautiful range of buildings, complete with granary and cartshed to the left, was unfortunately demolished soon after closure at the turn of the century.

Up until the middle of the last century Surrey had nearly fifty windmills; now there is only a handful left and of these only one, Outwood, still works. However, here are two which still survive. Shirley tower-mill, above, was the last large-scale windmill built in the county, in 1854. It worked until the end of the century and since then has been preserved in the grounds of a school. Lowfield Heath, on the other hand, had been allowed to fall into dereliction before any attempt was made at preservation. This entailed its movement and re-erection on the other side of Gatwick Airport where its restoration is now nearing completion at Charlwood.

The harvest has been safely gathered at Badshot Farm, Badshot Lea near Farnham, and now it is being built into well thatched ricks to protect it from any inclement weather before the threshing crew arrive. The elevator is powered by the horse gear in the foreground and the rick will be covered with the rick cloth, suspended from the poles, at night until the thatching is complete.

Lavender was one of the more unusual crops grown in Surrey in the areas around Mitcham, Beddington, Wallington, Carshalton, Sutton and Cheam, alongside chamomile and mint. The photograph was taken in Carshalton, where the oil of lavender was also distilled. Harvesting was done by itinerant pickers on their way to Kent for the hop-picking season.

Near Dorking, at Brockham and Betchworth, were extensive limeworks in pits in the chalk. These two scenes are at Brockham and show the kilns around 1938, some four years after lime burning had ceased and vegetation had begun to overtake the site. The horse and handler pause in more active days, while a rail wagon of the London, Brighton and South Coast Railway passes on the cable-hauled incline to the kilns.

A busy day at Gatwick racecourse as a horse is paraded in the ring before a large crowd. The racecourse became established here towards the end of the last century having been forced from its Croydon home by the spread of the town. It soon became one of the premier racecourses in the south of England, even having its own station on the nearby London, Brighton and South Coast Railway opened in 1891. From 1930, jockeys arriving by air used the newly opened adjoining aerodrome. The increasing popularity of this airfield ultimately led to the demise of the racecourse as, in 1936, this became the first Gatwick Airport. After the Second World War, flying from here was further increased when civilian aircraft returned and this led to the redevelopment of the airport on the racecourse and the closure of the old 'Beehive' building in 1958. The station for today's major international airport is built on the site of the racecourse station, and the only part of the racecourse now remaining is the bandstand, seen in the centre of the photograph, which has been re-erected in Crawley New Town.

Not really a workplace, but the family of six which occupied these huts in a charcoal burners' camp at the Chase in Haslemere always lived on the job, moving on when the supply of wood was exhausted. The photograph was taken on 16 August 1910.

These two men appear to be visitors as they are far too well dressed for this charcoal burners' camp near Westcott, *c*. 1900. Note the freshly cut wood to the left of the photograph, ready for the furnace.

The atmosphere around Mitcham must have been very polluted and unhealthy in the area's industrial heyday, for here there were vegetable oil distilleries, leather tanneries, and varnish works among others. Here are seen the appalling working conditions in one of the town's varnish works. The furnaces were coke fuelled and this can only have added to the noxious nature of the air.

An interior view of Blackburn's non-ferrous foundry at Catteshall Works, Godalming. The company was established in Guildford just before the Second World War as a general foundry and engineering works, moving from Godalming in 1987–8 to Dorset. In the photograph, taken in 1975, can be seen two crucible furnaces and piles of moulding boxes along with a selection of foundry tools on the walls.

A hoopshaver at his camp in Deerleap Woods, Wotton, at the turn of the century. He would have moved around the countryside from coppice to coppice in order to make the binding hoops for barrels in which to store dry-stuffs. The wood, usually hazel, was cut in spring and soaked in water before being riven. It was then placed in the brake, the tripod-like device to the left of the man, and shaved with a draw-knife. The hoops were then bent on an easel and the ends nailed to form a perfect circle.

Gathered in their workplace are the staff and management of A.B. Burton's Thames Ditton statue foundry on 28 May 1921 on the occasion of the visit of King George V. The statue behind them is of King Edward VII and was bound for New Delhi.

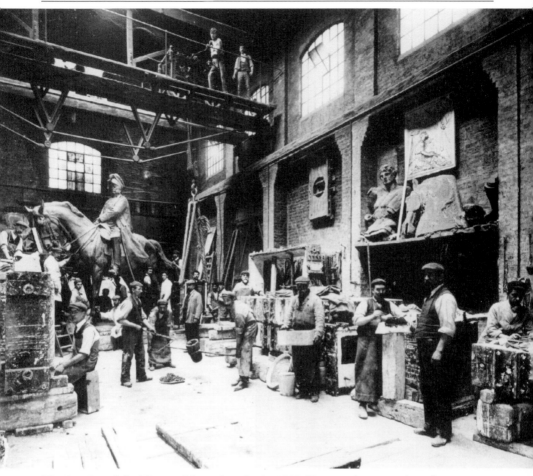

The interior of the Thames Ditton foundry in 1907. Two workmen are just about to pour molten metal from a crucible into a small mould in the centre of the photograph, while chasers are at work on a statue of the Duke of Cambridge by Adrian Jones which now stands in Whitehall, London. Overhead, two men are working the gantry crane to lift a mould box. This crane was the only part of the foundry to survive demolition in the 1970s. It was moved to the Rural Life Centre at Tilford, near Farnham, where it has been restored and re-erected by members of the Surrey Industrial History Group and can now be seen occasionally working again, fully man-powered. On the shelf to the right of the photograph are some of the many plaster patterns used in the production of G.F. Watts' 'Physical Energy' for Hyde Park.

The boilerman checks his charge at a Cobham brickworks. This was one of a number of brickfields in the area initially set up in 1782 to produce bricks for the rebuilding of Cobham Bridge. Later it is believed to have been used for burning London refuse, the ashes from which were utilized in the brick-production process.

Empty at the end of its useful life is the Guildford workhouse, the scene of much heartache over the years. This view shows the abandoned cells in 1966 just before demolition to make way for new building at St Luke's Hospital.

SECTION FOUR

The Working Man and Woman

Just some of the bricks used in the building of the Pollard's Hill residential development near Croydon, *c.* 1910. These were made in local brickworks especially set up to supply the builders. Benjamin Wilkinson is standing on the pile, while his uncle, another Benjamin, is pushing the left-hand barrow.

Stretching a chamois leather at Garrett Mills in Plough Lane, Wimbledon. The company was Chuter's, who occupied the premises from 1890 to 1960 in what was formerly a copper works.

Mr Rose, a gardener at Holcombe, Westcott, in the early 1900s, tends his charges in the greenhouse.

Two young lads from Farnham pause on a stile in Castle Hill after walking up from the town centre through some of the many hop gardens by which the town was surrounded. The hops here are growing on poles, a method which generally preceded the use of strings between rows of poles.

A break from harvesting in Clifton's Field, Reigate, in 1905. The reaper and binder seems to be undergoing some maintenance while the boys make the most of the interruption to rest their weary legs.

A Haslemere woman raises water from the well in her backyard on 7 October 1885. Not for her a long walk, for this is almost water on tap.

The postmen of Churt pose with the sub-postmaster outside his office and shop in the village. From the condition of the original photograph, it is obvious that it was a treasured possession which went everywhere with its owner.

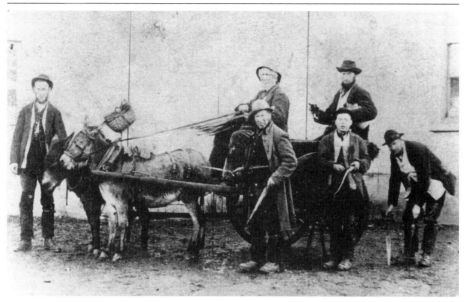

This photograph, taken outside the Golden Fleece public house in Elstead near Farnham around 1900, shows a group of local carrot diggers. They were renowned throughout the district for the speed with which they worked. Some extremely long straight carrots can be seen in the photograph, as can the special tools the gang used. The basket on the donkey harness is the workmen's lunch.

The hard way of harvesting, before the advent of labour-saving machines, is demonstrated by this reaper at Mitcham, c. 1870.

Two photographs taken at Westcott school around 1905. In the photograph top right Mr Chalke, the gardening master, gives a practical lesson in bee-keeping while the head-master, Mr Jackson, looks on. Above, an art class is in progress using chalk-boards. Note that the use of the left hand is being positively discouraged.

Another gardening class, this time at Bletchingley in 1911, tend the vegetable patch under the close supervision of the gentleman in the straw boater.

Former Prime Minister and farmer David Lloyd-George explains the principles of potato growing to visitors on his Bron-y-de, Churt estate near Hindhead in October 1934. The visitors were county councillors and farmers who had come to see the results of an experiment into the importance of fertilizer and manure in the growing of potatoes under the auspices of the Agricultural Committee of Surrey County Council.

Now illegal, but unfortunately still happening, badger digging was a popular pastime when this photograph was taken at Bletchingley Black Bushes in 1910. It was thought that badgers were disease carriers at this time and the original caption states, 'An army of men dug for two days and got out one badger.'

An AEC charabanc provides the transport for the James Knight and Sons' staff outing in the 1920s. The company were, and still are, drapers in Bell Street, Reigate, but where the coach was bound is not recorded.

An almost disappeared institution, especially in this part of the country, is the company sponsored brass band. This one was formed from the employees of Unwin Brothers' Gresham Press at Woking.

There cannot be many industries in which Surrey holds a monopoly, but here are four views of a factory unique to the county. This is the Royal British Legion poppy factory in Petersham Road, Richmond. Originating in the Old Kent Road, the industry moved here in 1926 when more room was needed. The first poppy day was held in 1921, when, for this year only, poppies were imported from France. Since that date the demand has grown and grown, and today the factory produces over 40 million annually and some 100,000 wreaths. After seventy years of continuous production, 120 personnel are employed full time along with some sixty outworkers.

German prisoners of war at work unloading timber from one of Harmsworth & Sons' narrow boats on the Basingstoke canal at Ash Vale during the First World War. Harmsworth's were boat builders of North Camp near Aldershot at this time, but later, in 1923, became the proud owners of the entire waterway for the princely sum of £5,000.

Alfred Hammond, on the left, and a colleague pause from moving gunpowder barrels at Chilworth gunpowder works in 1913. The entire operation was water powered until steam engines were introduced in the 1860s, and the millstream provided a safe and convenient means of transport within the works using flat-bottomed punts.

Wilfred Heasman, the miller at Coltsford Mill, Hurst Green, dresses the runner stone with a thrift and mill bill in February 1978, a task that has been performed here for centuries. Coltsford Mill is believed to be the last working watermill in Surrey.

Very little information is known about this photograph taken from an old glass lantern slide. It shows Cawley, the ratcatcher, complete with his team of dogs and his trusty donkey. What the bags contain defies the imagination.

A peaceful scene in the High Street at Bletchingley on 10 May 1907. The annual fair is in progress and a young girl is enjoying a donkey ride in the middle of what is now the main A25 road. The fair people's living vans are parked up on the left hand side of the road while the booths, including a coconut shy, are on the right.

The showman's engine is all sheeted up and the rides are still. The Haslemere fair is not yet open and the men are having a well earned rest as one of the womenfolk prepares the showmen's dinner in May 1911.

Collecting the mail at Redhill just after the turn of the century (right), the postman is waiting beside the Victorian pillar-box, while (below) Mrs W. Rose, a postwoman at Westcott during the First World War, delivers letters to No. 1 Westcott Street.

Setting off with the milk from Highcombe Farm in the Devil's Punchbowl in 1907 is George Mayes, the Hindhead milkman. Following the death of his mother, who is seen watching from the doorway, he lived here alone for a further thirty years until his own demise in 1939. Apart from a seven week spell in nearby Haslemere Hospital, he never ventured from the Hindhead area during his entire life.

Rake makers stop for a chat outside cottages in Betchworth during 1890. Their wares are leaning against the building, and include one very wide example.

Watching over a newly born charge and its mother is Mr Tanner, a shepherd at Abinger in the early years of this century. He carries a typical leg crook, probably made from old pipe or a gun barrel by the local blacksmith, and wears a sack around his waist. The fold is formed from hurdles with gorse piled up behind to protect the young lambs from foxes.

An agricultural labourer poses for the camera of his employer in the 1890s near Farnham. The employer was John Henry Knight, local landowner, farmer, banker and inventor. He was a keen amateur photographer and his photographs beautifully record the agricultural environment of his times, as well as the streets of the market town and his own inventions. These latter included a military catapult, the wood spring tyre, a brick-laying machine which unfortunately could not turn corners, and a motor car, possibly the first in Britain. He did, however, have the dubious honour of receiving the first speeding conviction in the country while motoring in Farnham's Castle Street.

Mr Potter, the Abinger blacksmith, stands at the door of his forge to observe the passing scene. Notice the iron tyre resting against the wall, the mandrell for shaping hoops for wheel hubs, and the smith's scrap heap to the left, a vital part of any village smithy.

The Bird family with their cart for deliveries outside the fishmongers and greengrocers shop they ran in Bletchingley around the turn of the century. Note the rail above the window from which meat and poultry could be hung for display.

The West Surrey General Benefit Society, formed in 1846, was just one of many friendly societies formed throughout the country to protect the working man and woman. Most are now long gone, having been largely amalgamated into the trade union movement, but in their day they served a vital purpose and, here, members from as far apart as Chertsey and Godalming pose proudly with their magnificent banner.

A potter at work at Wrecclesham, near Farnham in the 1870s. The photograph dates from soon after Absolom Harris founded his business in the village, and it is still in the hands of the same family today, producing traditional wares such as that seen here.

A group of shoppers pause on the way home with their wares to inspect the livestock at Guildford cattle market in Woodbridge Road.

The working man has always had to look his best, especially for the camera. One of the service industries catering to this need is that of the barber. Here we see one at work in a very rudimentary salon in the Bourne, Farnham. The gentleman receiving the trim is Harry Nixon; the effectiveness of the sheet covering his clothing seems very doubtful, unlike his need of a haircut. The man on the right appears, from the state of his scalp, to be an already satisfied customer, who came prepared with his own reading matter for the waiting room.

Doug Saunders, left, and Wally Dudley of Goodridge's outfitters in Farnham's Downing Street try on the 'bib-and-brace' overall especially made by the company for 'Tiny' Sawkins of Guildford Road in the town during 1958. Mr Sawkins was obviously a very large gentleman, not only in girth but also in height.

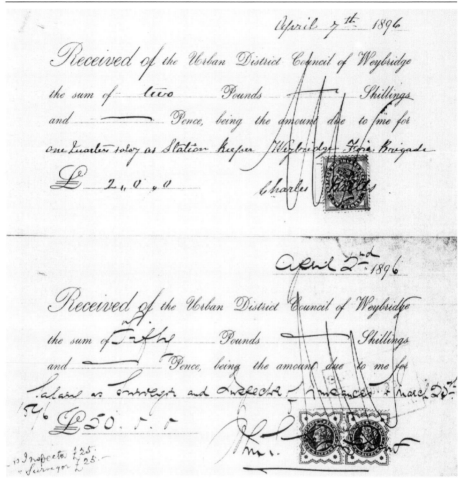

April 7th 1896

Received of the Urban District Council of Weybridge
the sum of ____two____ Pounds ____ Shillings
and ____ Pence, being the amount due to me for
one quarter salary as Station Keeper Weybridge Fire Brigade
£ 2 . 0 . 0   Charles

April 2nd 1896

Received of the Urban District Council of Weybridge
the sum of ____Fifty____ Pounds ____ Shillings
and ____ Pence, being the amount due to me for
salary as Surveyor and Inspector ... + March 25th
£50 . 0 . 0

" Inspector £25.
" Surveyor £25.

Two salary receipts for Weybridge UDC from April 1896 show a marked difference in remuneration. While the Fire Station Keeper received eight pounds per year, a Surveyor and Inspector got the princely sum of fifty pounds annually.

SECTION FIVE
Women at Work

Women have always worked of course, but for centuries they were restricted to what were regarded as the less physically and technically demanding jobs. Two world wars and numerous smaller conflicts changed all that for good. With the men fighting overseas, the ladies were drafted in to take their places, as a group of Vickers' machine-shop employees from Brooklands demonstrate during the First World War.

Here is another group of First World War women workers, but with a slightly more dangerous occupation. For many years gunpowder had been produced at Chilworth near Guildford. From the 1890s cordite was also manufactured here, and in 1915 a second cordite factory was built by the Admiralty. These are six of the many women employed here and they are wearing the issue uniform with the triangular crown-bearing badge of munitions workers.

Ladies from the Admiralty cordite factory and the Chilworth gunpowder works who formed a football team during the First World War. Some are wearing the navy blue ruched caps which formed part of their serge working uniform. Before the war the Chilworth Gunpowder Company fielded a cricket team and the workers also went on annual outings.

ASH

GUILDFORD RURAL DISTRICT COUNCIL

1829

This is to certify that

Mrs. I. Hawes

holds the position of Air Raid Warden and is authorised to carry out the duties of that office on behalf of the Council.

Clerk to the Council.

The Air Raid Warden's certificate issued to Mrs I. Hawes of Ash during the Second World War.

A washer-up at work in the British Restaurant in Kingston-upon-Thames. These were set up during the Second World War by local authorities to provide hot lunches for the populace.

The Farnham building firm of Crosby's became the largest door producer in Britain after the Second World War, making some 2½ million doors in 1972 alone. During the war, however, the factory was commandeered by the government for military production. The major item, as had been the case in the First World War, was ammunition packing, and here women are seen producing packing pieces for the boxes. Another large contract called for toilet seats for the War Department.

During the Second World War many vital industries were split up into smaller units in other factories and workshop buildings throughout the country. The reasons for this were twofold: firstly, to increase the total production capacity and, secondly, to prevent the loss of a large production unit by one bombing raid. Vickers set up dispersal depots throughout the county and here we see workers in one of the outstations 'somewhere in Surrey'.

Most of the dispersal depots were deliberately inconspicuous, perhaps just a watchman at the gate and a defence point. Many of the sites were in motor garages and workshops because with the petrol shortage there was little call for car servicing. The two shown here are Ben Stanley Ltd in Birwood Road, Hersham (above), and Oliver's Garage, Station Avenue, Walton-on-Thames. In both cases any reference to location has been removed from the buildings in order to confuse any potential invaders.

Women at work hoeing the vegetables on A.B. Johnson's New Park Farm at Cranleigh during the First World War. Mr Johnson was known locally as 'Top Spit Johnson' for his habit of buying up tracts of farmland and stripping the topsoil for sale as loam. The land was then sold on to builders for development and, as a result, many villagers now have gardens of almost pure clay and have to spend a small fortune on new topsoil.

It is easy to overlook the humble housewife who works seven days every week for no pay. Times have not always been so easy for her as today with many labour-saving tools. Women queue in Weybridge High Street during the food shortages of the First World War in 1916. They are hoping to purchase potatoes from Lock's greengrocery store before the supply runs out.

SECTION SIX
Keeping the Wheels Turning

The date is 4 December 1918 and the Sopwith Aviation works at Ham, Richmond, have suffered an electrical power failure. One of the company's steam wagons has been rapidly brought in to drive the factory line-shafting through the wall of the machine shop.

A contrast in transport types at Farnham. Two of Pharo's steam lorries, a Garrett and a Foden, stand in the yard, above, complete with crews, at Badshot Lea in 1923. Left to right in the photograph are Bill Pharo, Jean Pharo, Dick Pharo, George Pharo with S. Turner on the right making up what was otherwise a totally family affair. A later Foden stands well laden in Bear Lane in the town, below, with a delivery for Thomas Christy's toiletry works during the 1950s.

Two of Guildford Borough Council's dustmen proudly pose with their dustcart in Bedford Road on 30 August 1927. Six of these vehicles were brought by the corporation from Glover's of Warwick when refuse collections were started in 1905. This one is on its way to the Bedford Road Wharf where the refuse will be tipped into a barge for transport to the dump.

Bill Timperley operates the petrol pump at Wilkinson's Runfold Filling Station near Farnham, during the 1930s, for R. Hook's lorry, which has just left the sandpit located behind the pumps. This pit also belonged to Austin Wilkinson and a concrete tile making plant was established here. The latter was sold out to Redland Tiles in the 1950s.

Two stages in the development of an all-weather road surface are represented in these two photographs. Above, granite setts about to be laid in Quarry Street, Guildford, attracted a large crowd of spectators, while the hand tarring of the London to Worthing road in Ewell did not, perhaps because of the unpleasant odour. The date was Easter 1905 and crude coal-tar was being applied, in the same parish in which it was first used in the county in July 1901.

Sir Edwin Lutyens was the architect for the new Hampton Court bridge in the early 1930s along with Surrey County Council surveyor W.P. Robinson. The new bridge replaced a Victorian iron structure dating from 1865 which had become unsafe by 1923 and had a 10 m.p.h. speed limit imposed, ten years before the new bridge was opened. The entrance to Hampton Court Palace is in the upper right of the photograph.

Traffic, it seems, has always been a problem, with transport needing an ever increasing amount of space. Here we see grading work starting on the Farnham by-pass in 1938. Unfortunately, the Second World War intervened and the road was not finally opened until almost twenty years later.

The 1920s and '30s saw a number of by-passes built in Surrey, many of which are still in use today. The top two photographs on these pages show County Council steam shovels at work, on the left at Dorking in 1926, and at Guildford in 1933. The Guildford by-pass was paid for with money from the Work Fund set up by Mayor William Harvey in order

to relieve unemployment. This work also entailed the building of several bridges, bottom left, and the use of a narrow gauge railway to cut through the chalk ridge. Further east in the county, at Caterham, a diesel shovel is seen at work, bottom right, on the Caterham–Godstone by-pass, cutting through the same chalk escarpment.

Handley Page HP42 Heracles *Horatius* of Imperial Airways undergoes a pre-flight inspection at Croydon Airport in the mid-1930s. The famous control tower is to the left and a number of sightseers can be seen on the terminal roof.

A Bristol 170 Wayfarer transport aircraft is unloaded of its cargo of fruit and vegetables outside Gatwick's Beehive terminal in the late 1940s, closely watched by a policeman and customs officer.

For many years the only way of crossing the River Wey at St Catherine's near Guildford was by hand ferry. After a period without a ferryman, or woman as seen here in the 1860s, the National Trust, the owners of Shalford Meadows on the opposite bank, erected a footbridge to ease the crossing.

A crowded scene on the Thames at Richmond as some boats await customers while others undergo repair on the bank. The skiffs were also made here and at similar boat-houses at Weybridge.

A Wey barge of William Stevens and Sons of Guildford passes through Thames Lock at Weybridge during the 1950s. Two horses wait on the towpath to be reconnected once the vessel is through the lock.

The company produced their own barges at Dapdune Wharf, Guildford, and barge builder Ray Edwards is seen at work on *Perseverence IV* in 1934. He is assisted by J. White.

Two further photographs of the building of *Perseverence IV* at Dapdune Wharf. The first shows an earlier stage in the construction with the ribs seen to advantage. Below, in 1935, the vessel is launched sideways into the Wey Navigation from its building shed.

A tight fit for one of the last transformers made at the Hackbridge and Hewittic Electrical Company of Hersham as it passes under a railway bridge at Esher in 1972. The 240 MVA, 400/132 KV unit was bound for Wymondley near Hitchin in Hertfordshire.

Even after the end of the Second World War the Farnham firm of Crosby's continued to undertake some defence contracts. With their wide woodworking experience, the firm carried out such jobs as the repair of Bailey bridge pontoons in the 1950s.

A statue of General Buller from the Thames Ditton foundry completes the first part of its journey to Exeter. It is seen here on a Great Western Railway horse waggon on arrival at Paddington Station in 1905. Notice the very small front wheels on the waggon.

Barges clog the channel of the Wey Naviation at Weybridge during the General Strike of 1928.

The crew of this locomotive prepare to remount their charge after filling the tanks from the water crane at Guildford Station in the 1950s.

Guildford Roundhouse just two months before its closure in July 1967 in a painting by Surrey Industrial History Group Patron David Shepherd. The locomotive shed was situated in an old chalk pit at the foot of Farnham Road and, in its day, was a very busy place. It is seen again below in an altogether more sorry state during demolition in 1968. The site has now been redeveloped as a 'shed' for road transport in the form of the Farnham Road multi-storey car park, a sign of the times perhaps.

Surrey has the distinction of having the world's first purpose-built banked racing track at Brooklands, now sadly disused and partly removed. It was built by Hugh Locke-King on his Weybridge estate starting in October 1906. The lower photograph shows levelling of the track in December of that year. This involved diverting the River Wey in three places and cutting through a natural hill. Around 300,000 cubic yards of earth had to be moved and two tunnels and three bridges built. The cost of all this work, which took a mere nine months to complete, was £150,000, and the banked track, above, became a famous landmark.

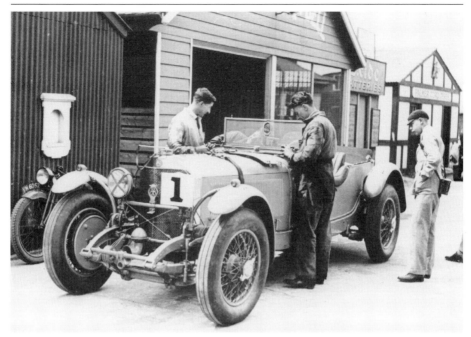

Two workshop scenes at the Brooklands circuit: that above shows Malcolm Campbell's Mercedes-Benz 38/250 being worked on around 1931 and, below, a mechanic is engaged in rebuilding an ERA engine.

Crews and vehicles of the Victoria Transport Company of Farnham line up for the photographer before setting off for the day's tasks. The company were general removers as well as being employed transporting sand and gravel from the pits which surrounded the town. The firm is no longer in existence and the yard now forms part of the Central Car Park in Victoria Road.

The delivery fleet of Tice's outside the Badshot Lea Kiln around 1938. All the vehicles, including the tractors, are Fords. Daily deliveries were made to local shops and the London markets. With the vehicles are, left to right, Jim Bradley, Joseph Power, Alf Butler, farm foreman Bill Bright, Charlie Crumplin, -?-, and Len Lucas, while in the top doorway of the kiln stands 'Lion' Kray with Tom Morton below him.

From the days of the earliest messenger with his forked stick, the mail has always been delivered with the utmost speed. These two photographs indicate how that speed has increased. Above is seen a Royal Mail parcel waggon outside Guildford Post Office in North Street. The cipher on the side is ER which dates the photograph to the 1900s. The mail van below is standing outside the Customs House at Croydon Airport in 1933 having delivered mail for an outgoing flight. Notice the air-mail signs on the van's roof.

The postman seems well pleased with the service he has just received at this bicycle shop near Farnham. All the cycles have pneumatic tyres, but most have only a single brake. Note the BSA advertisement in the left hand window.

Mr Bodle, the Abinger wheelright, and an assistant shrink a tyre to fit a wheel they have just made, on the tyring platform outside the village workshop.

January 1926 was generally wet and mild with only a cold spell in the middle of the month, so this must have been a freak snowstorm at Banstead on the 27th. However, this family were obviously ready for anything and are certainly well equipped for their shopping trip to the post office through what were described locally as the Banstead 'steppes'.

A local officer's Rolls-Royce gets the five-star treatment at Abbott's garage at Wrecclesham, Farnham. To judge from the interest being shown, the Lucas Beam Setter was a comparatively new gadget at the time.

SECTION SEVEN

Accidents will Happen

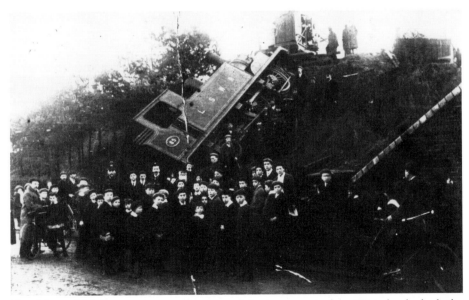

The driver of this locomotive on a Saturday night theatre train from Waterloo had a lucky escape at Camberley in the early 1900s. The tank engine, an 0–4–4 No. 65 of the London South Western Railway, went off the embankment when it hit the buffers on a siding after the driver became confused and thought he was still on the main line. A large crowd has gathered on the following morning to watch the recovery operation get under way.

Another evening railway accident, this time at Peasmarsh near Guildford on 9 September 1873. The Portsmouth express was approaching the town when it struck a bullock that had broken loose while being driven from Guildford Market. The engine and tender stayed on the rails but all ten carriages were flung off, killing three passengers. The driver managed to run his locomotive on to Guildford station to summon help and, as a result of the accident, events were set in motion which led to the introduction of the communication cord and interconnecting brakes.

Firemen in Second World War dress, complete with steel helmets, pump petrol from damaged rail tanker wagons at Shalford Station on 11 April 1944. Following an accident, some had overturned and caught fire. The driver, Arthur Griffen, showed great bravery in dividing the burning train and moving the front part to safety. For this action he later received an award. It prevented a total loss of what was, at the time, a vital commodity. Following the accident, engineers were called in to repair abutments on the nearby A281 roadbridge damaged by expansion of the girders in the intense heat.

This Burrell steam engine, No. 2243 of Richardson's from Epsom, was involved in a fatal accident after it ran away in Epsom Road, Guildford, during February 1911, while delivering furniture to Southampton. Note the collection of bicycles and one tricycle brought along by the sightseers.

The aftermath of an exciting night on the Hog's Back near Guildford on 25 April 1974. This is all that was left of a British Oxygen Company lorry loaded with acetylene cylinders which caught fire at about 2.15 a.m. The driver, a Mr Rankin of Crawley, noticed a wheel on fire, attempted to extinguish it with his windscreen-washer bottle but failed. He warned gypsies living nearby and undoubtedly saved some lives as two caravans were damaged in the ensuing fire and explosions. Firemen from Farnham, Guildford and Aldershot attended the incident but could not prevent half the load exploding. The road was closed all the following morning to allow clearing up of the debris and repairs to the road surface.

All towns have their fair share of road accidents; some areas have their real 'black spots'. These four photographs are all from the Farnham area, where the narrow main road through Wrecclesham village is one such place. Above is seen a Royal Flying Corps lorry which partially demolished a house there on 3 May 1916. Another lorry went shopping at the Pet Stores in the town's East Street during the 1930s. A policeman guards the scene and the load has been supported with timber baulks until the vehicle can be recovered.

Ice and snow always seem to cause trouble, even for the US Army whose 'wrecker', above, is seen embedded in the International Meat Company shop in Downing Street, Farnham, in 1947. Aldershot and District Traction Company No. 15 bus also seems to be somewhat delayed by the weather in Alma Lane, Heath End, during the 1950s.

The London printing company of Unwin's established a branch factory at Chilworth near Guildford in 1871. Production continued here until a disastrous fire in November 1895, the aftermath of which is shown in the photograph above. After the fire the company moved to a former paper mill at Old Woking. Below is seen the company's own fire brigade, believed to be at the Woking Plant. Whether this had been in existence before the fire is not known; perhaps it was formed as a result of the unfortunate occurrence.

A fireman damps down the smouldering remains of Gates' Dairy in Guildford High Street, c. 1900, after a fire which also severely damaged the Three Pigeons public house next door.

Cable and Reeks' shop, also in Guildford High Street, was destroyed by fire during the First World War on 5 November 1915. Some enterprising individual saw the possibility of using the resulting scene of devastation to make a representation of conditions in the trenches of the Western Front and open it to the paying public. This even included the building of the replica windmill seen in the background.

St Catherine's School for girls at Bramley, near Godalming, caught fire during a thunder-storm on 11 April 1907. Eyewitnesses described the building being struck by a fireball, but fortunately most of the pupils were away for the Easter holidays. Guildford and Godalming brigades attended but were hampered by a water shortage.

Reigate firemen carry out hose-cart drill during a competition around 1922 at the old Guildford market site at Woodbridge Road.

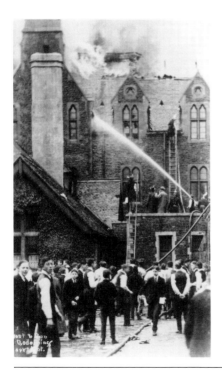

Just after 8 a.m. on Friday 19 March 1918 a pupil of Verite House at Charterhouse School, Godalming, discovered a fire on the upper floor of the building. It had been caused by an electrical fault in the roof, and despite the best efforts of both house and school fire brigades along with appliances from Godalming, Guildford, Woking and Kingston among other brigades, the fire caused much damage. This was due at least in part to a shortage of water which had to be pumped up from the river, and it was not until the middle of the afternoon that the fire was brought under control. Not one pupil was injured during the fire though many had to endure the hardship of sleeping in a large marquee in the garden throughout the summer while the debris was removed and the accommodation rebuilt.

Quite what happened to this car in Camberley is unknown and one wonders if it was a write-off. It was probably a local vehicle as it carries a Surrey registration.

Guildford Town Bridge at the foot of the High Street was virtually demolished during the floods of 1900. The bridge, which had survived many storms over the years, finally succumbed after timber from John Moon's yard upstream was washed against the piers and prevented the flood waters getting away. Today the replacement bridge, itself unable to cope with the weight of passing traffic, is restricted to pedestrians only.

This lorry tumbled into the building site it was serving in Portsmouth Road, Guildford, in 1967 during the building of a retaining wall. Despite attempts to recover it with the mechanical digger shown here, a mobile crane had eventually to be brought in to salvage the miraculously little-damaged vehicle.

A sad scene at Brooklands in 1932 during the British Racing Drivers' Club 500 mile race. The driver of this four-litre Bentley, uprated to eight litres capacity, Clive Dunfree, was killed. Travelling at 126 m.p.h., he went too high on the banking while passing Earl Howe's Bugatti and put a wheel over the edge.

SECTION EIGHT
It Pays to Advertise

FROM

FREDERICK WILLIAM FRANCIS ANNETT

Picture Frame Maker,

CARPENTER, ✢ JOINER, ✢ UNDERTAKER,

House Painter and Decorator,

HERSHAM, SURREY.

ESTIMATES GIVEN FOR GENERAL REPAIRS.

Window Blinds of every description made to order.

AGENT FOR THE SUN FIRE AND LIFE OFFICE.

Mr Annett didn't like to move too far away from his former comrades when he left the services, so he set up salons in military camps around the Surrey-Hampshire border. These included York Road at Camberley where, as his training would have taught him, officers do not like to mix with the 'other ranks'.

THE CORPORATION OF REIGATE

DESIRE TO BRING BEFORE YOUR NOTICE

The Reduction in Rates and the ❧ ❧

Advantages of

❧ ❧ ELECTRIC LIGHTING.

For this purpose they have appointed a Commercial Agent who is qualified to advise you as to the latest and best methods of deriving the greatest advantages from its use, and of answering any questions that may arise.

The obvious advantages over any other Artificial Illuminant are :—

(1). It is Cheaper.

(2). It is Healthier.

(3). It is Cleaner.

(4). It is Safer.

(5). It is the most Convenient.

(6). It Preserves your Decorations.

The Price is now reduced to a uniform rate of 5½d. per unit for Lighting, and 2d. per unit for Power and Radiator purposes.

This will bring it within the reach of all, and the Corporation are desirous of assisting and advising prospective consumers. All enquiries addressed to the Electricity Works will receive prompt attention.

Yours faithfully,

W. S. ROSS,

Borough Electrical Engineer.

Right: When this beer advertisement was published a strong selling point was a chemical analysis of the product as well as commendations as to its taste.

It appears that electricity was still something of a novelty in Reigate around 1927 when the handbill, left, was issued. At about the same time the staff were photographed in the generating station off Wray Common Road. Although the steam-powered generating station had been opened at a cost of £34,000 in 1901 electricity was obviously not a top seller. The motive power was later changed to diesel, presumably because of the increased demand due at least in part to this campaign. Later, around 1934, the Central Electricity Board took over the supply to the town.

ESTABLISHED 300 YEARS.

TRADE   MARK.

"BLESSINGS OF YOUR HEART, YOU BREW GOOD ALE."—Shakespeare.

ABSOLUTELY PURE ALE.   ABSOLUTELY PURE ALE.

HODGSON'S KINGSTON BREWERY CO., Ltd.

Brew only from—The Finest Growth of Hops—The Choicest Malts - The Purest Water.

(From the Famous **ARTESIAN WELL** situate on their own Premises).   THERE IS NO BETTER BREWED IN THE UNITED KINGDOM.

The High Reputation of

HODGSON'S INDIA PALE ALE

HAS STOOD THE TEST OF UPWARDS OF A CENTURY.

The Famous **BROWN BEER OF BURTON** was drunk for full three centuries before the **BITTER BEERS OF HODGSON**, and Allsopp, and Bass, came into vogue.—See Leading Article *Daily Telegraph*, February 11th, 1887.   **HODGSON'S BITTER** has long been known and appreciated by riverside men.

REPORT OF DR. OTTO HEHNER.

President of the Society of Public Analysts.

"I have made full and exhaustive analyses of the Ale brewed by **HODGSON'S KINGSTON BREWERY COMPANY**, Limited, and of the water used at the Brewery.

"I find the Ale to be of the most excellent quality; indeed, I do not think it could in any way be surpassed. It is thoroughly well brewed of Malt and Hops only, and is splendid as to soundness, strength and taste.

"The water supply is very good and pure, and in every way suited for the production of good High-Class Ales."

REPORT OF DR. T. REDWOOD,
Ph.D., F.C.S., F.J.C.,

Professor of Chemistry and Pharmacy.

"I have carefully examined, tested, and analysed the India Pale Ale produced by **HODGSON'S KINGSTON BREWERY COMPANY**, and also a sample of the water used in its production. The Ale partakes of the character of the well-known Burton Ales. It is of excellent flavour, clean to the palate, and of high alcoholic strength. These qualities may to some extent be ascribed to the use of a water well suited to the brewing of this class of Ale, but there is also evidence of its being produced from finest malt and hops, and no evidence of any hop-substitute having been used."

ABSOLUTELY PURE ALE.

VERY DESIRABLE FOR   **PRIVATE FAMILIES.**

	In Casks of 4½ Gals.	9 Gals.	18 Gals.			In Casks of 4½ Gals.	9 Gals.	18 Gals.
FAMILY PALE ALE, FPA	4/6	9/-	18/-	PORTER, P		4/6	9/-	18/-
TABLE BITTER ALE, TBA	5/3	10/6	21/-	SINGLE STOUT, SS		6/-	12/-	24/-
INDIA PALE ALE, IPA	6/3	12/6	25/-	DOUBLE STOUT, DS		7/6	15/-	30/-
BEST BITTER ALE, BA	7/6	15/-	30/-	KEEPING STOCK ALE, KA		8/3	16.6	33/-

DISCOUNT for CASH ONLY, 1s. per 18 Gallons; 6d. per 9 Gallons.

BOTTLED ALES.

A BOTTLING DEPARTMENT having been OPENED at this Brewery, Customers can be Supplied with Bottled Ales and Stout of the Finest Quality-

					Per doz. Imp. Pints.
PALE ALE					4/-
INDIA PALE ALE					3 -
DINNER ALE					2/6
K. STOUT					2/6
STOUT					4/-

In Corked or Patent Screw-Stoppered Bottles, as desired.

HODGSON'S KINGSTON BREWERY CO., LIMITED, KINGSTON-ON-THAMES,

139

BROCKHAM, SURREY,

With Siding to the S.E. & C. Railway.

Catalogue of the whole of the

BRICK-MAKING PLANT

INCLUDING

Brickmaking Machines by Whitaker & Co., Wire Cut Machines, Grinding Mills with Elevators,

STEAM ENGINE AND MACHINERY,

20 H.P. ENGINE by Clayton & Shuttleworth,

WITH TRAVELLING WHEELS,

6 H.P. VERTICAL ENGINE by Garret & Son,

Shafting. Driving Wheels, &c., Pumps, 2 Brick Presses, Iron Winding Gear,

LEATHER AND OTHER DRIVING BANDS,

Railway Track & Narrow Gauge Ditto & Waggons,

TRADE BUILDINGS

13 Circular Kilns, Brick Shaft 100-ft. high, Machine and other Sheds, Portable Offices, Barrows, Trucks, Implements, large quantity Old Iron, and about

350,000 BRICKS,

and numerous other items appertaining to the Business, which Messrs.

PEAT & HOLDSWORTH

are favoured with instructions from the Directors of the Brockham Brick Company, Limited, to sell by Auction on the Premises, about 1½ miles from Betchworth Station, in consequence of the lease of this yard having expired,

On MONDAY, 10th OCTOBER, 1910,

Brockham Brickworks were located between the 'Pilgrims' Way' and the railway line to which they had their own siding. It seems that the works did not find a buyer as this marked the end of brickmaking at the site, and today the clay pit is flooded and used for fishing.

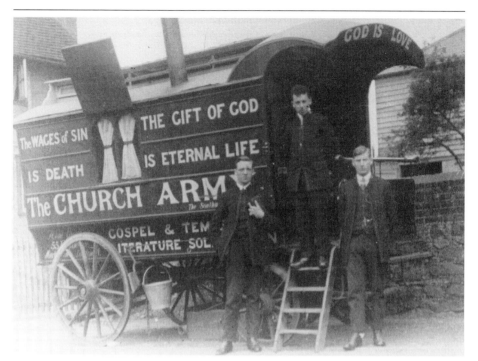

Twenty years separate these two photographs of religious missions in the county. Above, three preachers of the Southwark Diocesan Church Army with their horse-drawn caravan were bringing the word of the Lord to Bletchingley in June 1914. Rather less is known of the Austin Six van portrayed by Reigate photographer Harry Snook around 1930, but it appears, like the vehicle above, to be in pristine condition.

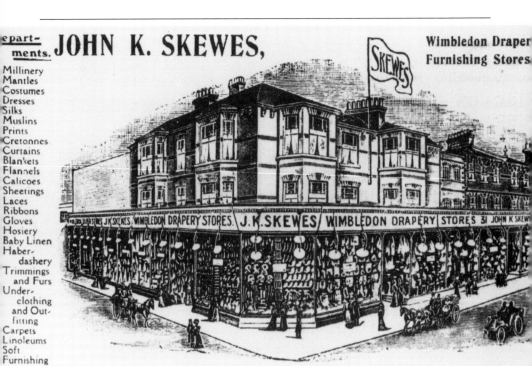

JOHN K. SKEWES,

Wimbledon Draper
Furnishing Stores

epart-
ments.
Millinery
Mantles
Costumes
Dresses
Silks
Muslins
Prints
Cretonnes
Curtains
Blankets
Flannels
Calicoes
Sheetings
Laces
Ribbons
Gloves
Hosiery
Baby Linen
Haber-
dashery
Trimmings
and Furs
Under-
clothing
and Out-
fitting
Carpets
Linoleums
Soft
Furnishing

lephone No. 81 Nat. Wimbledon.
legrams: "Skewes, Wimbledon."

Broadway and Gladstone Road, Wimbledon, S

A crowded window display seems to have been a feature of Skewes' drapery stores at Wimbledon. There is a truly impressive list of departments in this 1907 advertisement and it is interesting to note the out-of-scale figures in the drawing, designed to make the shop look all the more grand.

Modesty was obviously not a fault of Cheel and Company of Guildford High Street. The sign in the window advertises the company's own Guildford tobacco mixture which appears to have received royal patronage.

R. WINSKELL & Co.,

GLASS, LEAD, OIL and COLOUR MERCHANTS,

98, High Street, MERTON, and
1, Haydon's Road, WIMBLEDON.

Sashes Primed and Glazed.

Winskell's staff pose outside their shop in Merton. From the sign it appears that their varnish was made in Wolverhampton and not at one of the many local varnish works.

Monoplanes at Brooklands, Weybridge. A.S. No. 117.

An aerodrome was soon established within the Brooklands racing circuit, and it was here that the first British-designed heavier-than-air craft flew, with A.V. Roe at the controls, in 1908. By the end of 1910 no less than five flying schools were in business with a further five following by 1912. This made Brooklands the centre of flying training for the country with 318 out of a total of 664 pupils who received instruction from civilian schools obtaining it here at Weybridge. Included among them was Mrs Hilda Hewlett, who gained certificate No. 122 on 29 July 1911 to become the first British woman pilot.

DEPERDUSSIN MONOPLANES.

£450 complete, as used by W. H. EWEN across Firth of Forth.

AVIATION SCHOOL AT BROOKLANDS.

Special Terms to Army and Navy Officers.

APPLY TO—

THE BRITISH DEPERDUSSIN AEROPLANE SYNDICATE, LTD.,

30, REGENT STREET, PICCADILLY CIRCUS,

Telephone: 180 GERRARD.   LONDON, S.W.   Wire "SANTOCHIMO, LONDON.'

Two advertisements for Brooklands flying schools are shown here. Both Vickers and the Deperdussin School were established in 1912, Vickers continuing at the site as manufacturers, and finally acquiring the entire circuit and airfield in 1946.

VICKERS
FLYING SCHOOL
Brooklands.

Pupils are taught to fly Monoplane and Biplane.

Sole licensees in the United Kingdom and the Colonies for
LEVASSEUR PROPELLERS.

Prices of trial propellers upon application.

VICKERS Limited,
Aviation Department,
Vickers House, Broadway,
Westminster, S.W.

R. BIGSWORTH,

(Late 15th Hussars,)

HAIRDRESSER, PERFUMER & TOBACCONIST.

SEPARATE ROOMS FOR OFFICERS.

GENERAL OUTFITTER.   Suits made to order.

5 York Road and Royal Engineers' Camp, Aldershot,

and Bordon Camp, Hants.

Trooper Bigsworth didn't like to move too far away from his former comrades when he left the services, so he set up salons in military camps around the Surrey-Hampshire border. These included York Road at Camberley where, as his training would have taught him, officers do not like to mix with the 'other ranks'.

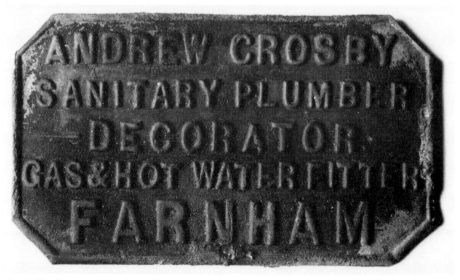

Crosby's, the large Farnham door manufacturing company, had a much humbler beginning when the founder, Andrew Crosby, started up as a plumber and decorator in 1877. Even then, however, he recognized the power of advertising, and all the cold water tanks he installed carried this plaque. The efficacy of this campaign must be in some doubt as most of the tanks were of course fitted in lofts; nonetheless, the firm went on to much greater things.

TO MILLERS.

HEASMAN'S

MILLSTONE TRAM STAFF

FOR PROVING MILLSTONES

Enables the Miller to staff his Stones more accurately than is possible by the old method with the long staff by hand. It can be adjusted to take the Stone down at eye or breast, or perfectly straight, to suit any trade or opinion. As all Millstones have a tendency to wear on two opposite sides (or, as practical Millers term "winding"), this machine will shew the exact part of the Stone where the Miller should use the bill more freely, so as to reduce it to that exact face as will enable him to clean every particle of flour from the offal with less pressure of Stone; consequently, a great saving of power is effected, and a much richer and stronger quality of flour produced.

William Heasman thought he was on to a winner when he took out this advertisement for his Millstone Tram Staff. How successful he was is not recorded, but a Wilfred Heasman was still in business as the miller at Coltsford Mill, Hurst Green, in 1978.

Glovers' soap was made in Mitcham, but if they were still in business today the Advertising Standards Authority would probably have something to say about their style. The different types produced are listed on the washerwoman's skirt.

A very upmarket newspaper delivery boy in Farnham. His vehicle provided plenty of space for advertising W.H. Smith and Son whose shop, at that time, was located in South Street. The tricycle is equipped with acetylene lamps supplied from centrally mounted gas generators both front and rear.

THE UP-TO-DATE FLEET OF THE
Pearl Grey Coaches, Ltd
North Street, Guildford.

A fine line-up of charabancs of the Pearl Grey Coach company in North Street, Guildford, awaiting passengers for trips to the seaside. Groups from pubs, factories and church organizations were the most likely customers.

In the seventeenth century, when coinage was in short supply, many traders issued their own currency in the form of trade tokens. They were used as change for transactions and each token was worth one farthing, being exchangeable as currency at other businesses in the local area. The issuers used this opportunity to advertise their wares and services, and, on the left, is one from Thomas Wilmot, a carrier of Shalford 'neere Guildford'. Chandler 'Henery Bradfoulde' of Godalming issued the other token, showing candles being dipped, in 1657. One of the last remnants of the token system was the use of milk tokens, represented by one below from the Guildford and District Industrial Co-operative Society.

SECTION NINE
Technology's Edge

After the Second World War Hawker Aircraft took over the former bomber base of Dunsfold Aerodrome. Here they set up an aircraft assembly line, eventually becoming Hawker Siddeley Aviation before merging with BAC to form British Aerospace. It was at Dunsfold that the company produced the most revolutionary aircraft design to be seen since the war, the world-beating Harrier. All test flying on the vertical take-off and landing aircraft and its predecessor, the Kestrel, was carried out here. The Harrier also became the first post-war aircraft to be sold to the United States military services, and here US Marine Corps AV-8A aircraft are seen in production during 1970.

When Gatwick Airport was built on the site of the former flying school of Home Counties Aircraft Services, next to the racecourse, during the 1930s, it was to a very innovative design. The British Airports Authority made a great point, when opening the new North Terminal in 1988, of the fact that it was the first satellite-type airport building in Britain. This seems very strange when sitting not more than a few hundred yards away was the true holder of this title. The 'Beehive', as it became known, was able to accept aircraft on all sides and passengers arrived through a tunnel from a specially built station on the nearby Brighton railway line. The line of the tunnel can be seen to the right of this photograph, cutting across the taxiways. The building also had telescoping covered walkways from the departure and arrival gates which were run out to the aircraft in order to protect the passengers from any inclement weather.

The Beehive nearing completion in 1936, with the telescopic walkways in position on their rails but awaiting the weatherproof skinning. The large panoramic windows of the lounge and restaurant are clearly visible, as is the centrally mounted control tower. The building is still in existence and serves today as offices.

The new airport in use on 25 July 1936 as a British Airways de Havilland DH86 prepares to depart on the inaugural night mail service to Germany watched by a small group of officials.

Robins' removers were fully occupied at the time this photograph was taken with the arrival of town gas in Farnham. Iron pipes for the mains were delivered by rail to the station goods yard (note the goods shed in the background). The company's steam lorry fleet, complete with trailers, collected them for delivery to the road gangs around the town. The gasworks were situated off East Street in an area now occupied by small industrial units and the sports centre.

A short-lived experiment launched at Ockley Green on 2 August 1973 was the Dorking–Coldharbour–Ockley postbus service. This seems more appropriate to the Scottish Highlands than rural Surrey. Present at the launch were Virginia McKenna and Bill Travers.

Two photographs to mark the beginning and end of an era. That above shows the laying of tram tracks for electric traction at Brixton around 1895, while below is the last tram service leaving the Norwood depot on 6 April 1952. Trams from here operated in Brixton and Kennington. After Norwood's demise it was not long before the last tram ran anywhere in the capital, on 5 July of the same year.

Workmen proudly display a monstrous wooden propeller at Lang's Riverside Works, Addlestone. From left to right they are J.D. Titler the General Manager, I. Martin inspector, H. Tibbs painter, R. Drew and J. Vincent carpenters, H. Atkins and W. Bragg metal workers, and S. Thorne the Chief Inspector.

At the end of the Second World War, the Airscrew Company, which had taken over Lang's, ceased propeller production at their Weybridge Trading Estate works, and the staff are seen mourning the demise with a mock burial. The company subsequently produced chipboard at the site under the trade name of 'Weyroc'.

Stonebridge Wharf at Shalford between Guildford and Godalming in 1915. Here, besides the timber, gunpowder from the nearby Chilworth mills is being loaded onto barges with the help of the treadmill crane on the right. The wharf is situated at the junction of the Wey and Arun Canal with the Wey Navigation.

Another treadmill crane, this time at Guildford Wharf, is demonstrated by Harry Stevens, the owner of the Wey Navigation. This particular example was saved from destruction and moved to its present position adjacent to the Town Bridge in Guildford.

Hubert Booth established the British Vacuum Cleaner Company in 1901. This later became Goblin (BVC) Ltd and moved to Leatherhead in 1938, continuing business there until 1984. Originally the machines were sold, partly at least, on their value to health. These are the results of tests carried out on dust from Marlborough House during the early part of the century, conducted by Prof. Stanley Kent of Bristol University. The figures must have seemed quite alarming to the general public at the time.

Henry Jackson demonstrates the mulch roller he designed as Nursery Manager for Tilhill Forestry at Tilford. The machine, attached to a Ferguson tractor, was used to recover the polythene mulch used around seedlings in the nursery which, until that time, had been discarded.

A rather dubious first for the county was that of having the first crematorium to be built in Britain. This was constructed in Hermitage Road, Woking, during 1878. However, due to ambiguities with the law it was not used until 1884. The photograph is taken from a postcard issued at the time, though the idea that anyone would have wished to record their visit here in this way seems a little strange to say the least.

Acknowledgements

The production of this book would not have been possible without the help, interest and support of many people and organizations. Not least among these are the members of the SIHG, without whose encouragement the volume would not have been started. To them must go the credit for the lion's share of the actual collecting of the images used. I should like to thank them and everyone else who has supplied photographs or helped with information, all of whom are listed below. To anyone I have omitted go my sincere apologies, and likewise to those whose pictures have not actually appeared. Hopefully, this will be rectified in any future volume.

Alf Adley • Jackie Andrews • Bill Bailey • David Barker • Nell Basting
Bourne Hall Museum • British Wax Refining Co. • Brooklands Museum
Mr A.O. Brown • Bob Coomes • Shirley Corke and Abinger Hammer Women's Institute
Glenys Crocker • Elmbridge Museum • Elphicks of Farnham
Judie English • Farnham Museum • Peter Finch, Nutfield Local History Group
S.E.D. Fortescue • Ivy Gale • Goodness Gracious, Ockley • Goodridge's Outfitters, Farnham
Mike Goolding • Guildford Institute of the University of Surrey • Guildford Museum
Mrs L.K. Hammond • Mr A. Hammond
Peter Harris of the Wandle Industrial Museum • R. Hartnup • Mike Hayter
Dr Alan Ingram • Henry Jackson and Rural Life Centre, Tilford
Mrs D. Johnson, Mrs N. Machell and Banstead History Group • Monica Jones
John King and Croydon Airport Society • Kingston Heritage Centre
Gordon Knowles, Leatherhead and District Local History Society • Nora Leach • John Linsey
Tony Martin • Deryck Moore, Bletchingley Conservation and Historical Society • Gerry Moss
National Trust – Wey Navigation • Rowena Oliver • Roger Packham • Alan Paine Ltd
Jean Parratt • Michael Pitchers • Bob Power • Gerry Price • Royal British Legion Poppy Factory
Muriel Shaw and Peter Burgess of Croydon NHSS
David Shepherd • Ron Shettle Fire Brigades of Surrey Preservation Trust
David Smith • Mrs E. Stevens • Derek Stidder • Surrey Archaeological Society
Surrey Local Studies Library • Surrey Record Office • Malcolm Tadd
Peter Tarplee • University of Surrey AVA Unit • Richard Unwin
Ann Wheeler of Charterhouse School

Animals also played their part. Jack wandered the platforms of Reigate station collecting for the Railwaymen's Homes.